Revelations from Genesis

The Untold Biblical Story of Creation

Who Cain Feared and Where They Came From

Study material:

King James Version of the Bible– KJV

New King James Version of the Bible – NKJV

Strong's Analytical Concordance – SAC

Strong's Blue Letter Bible - SBLB

Revelations from Genesis
The Untold Biblical Story of Creation
Who Cain Feared and Where They Came From

Prologue:

After murdering his only brother in a field out of anger and jealousy, then being confronted by God, the creator of all things, Cain had the audacity to dismiss his brother's absence. Then he turned and questioned God. "Am I my brother's keeper?" he asked.

In a matter of moments, in the blink of an eye, as Cain inhaled his next breath, he was put on trial, judged, found guilty, and sentenced. Then he exhaled.

Still, Cain remained unremorseful and could only think of one thing, himself. He made no effort to defend his actions because he could not. His only response was: woe is me!

"My punishment is greater than I can bear," he cried. Thinking nothing of the brother he slew, he continued with his plea. "Behold, thou hast driven me out this day from the face of the earth, and from thy face shall I be hid, and I shall be a fugitive and a vagabond in the earth, and it shall come to pass, that every one that finds me shall slay me."

These eight words spoken by Cain, 'every one that finds me shall slay me,' has lead to a question that has amazingly remained unanswered for centuries. Who was Cain referring to that could possibly find and slay him? Indeed there are many answers offered, but none that make sense, and none will ever make sense until those attempting to answer understand creation as recorded by Moses—and not the story of creation as told by those who first interpreted Moses' account.

Since there was only Adam, Eve, and Cain on the earth, who could Cain have possibly been referring to? Had he gone mad? Was he hallucinating? Was he thinking of possibilities off into the future when his mother and father would have more children; thus presenting a threat from his own siblings?

I guess when you start off with the wrong question you will inevitably come to the wrong conclusion. The right question should be, why is it we do not know who the people were that Cain feared, and where they came from? Since the Bible clearly tells us who Cain feared why then is that even a question to begin with? This most certainly will come as a shock to the reader, but sadly the account of creation we have all believed is not even written in the scriptures. At least, not exactly as it is recorded.

The story of God creating a man, and putting him in a garden, then creating a woman, starting the human race, is so commonplace that it is not even questioned; but what if we got it wrong? What if we read the story wrong, and it actually happened a little differently, but we just never took notice? What if your Bible actually tells a different story from what you believe it says? What if we just got the creation story wrong?

About the Author:

Born in April of 1970, in Birmingham England, I was the second to last of 7 children; five girls and two boys. We grew up in a small, modest home on Onibury Road in Handsworth. As a family we all attended church, and never missed Sunday school, nor Sunday service. At least not one that I can remember. You would find us at Gibson Road Church every Sunday morning, into the early afternoon. However, my dad never attended church services back then; it was only us kids and my mother.

Sadly, when I was around nine, my parents divorced, and my mother left with our youngest sister to come to America. It was a really strange time for me when my mother left. It seemed as though God left with her. No more church services and no more families over for Sunday dinner after service. It was a house that now felt cold since it was emptied of any religious activity.

It took many years for me to see, but although my mother left physically, she never really left us alone. She prayed for us continually, and so whenever I look back at my childhood, one of the things I see is how God was still there working in my life. Not that everything turned out perfect, it certainly did not. Yet even with some very unfortunate events, I can still see where God worked.

In 1983, at age thirteen, my mother brought me to America as she was trying to, and in the end managed to, bring us all here. Even so God was still only a memory in the back of my mind. An experience I had, but no longer an experience I was having. Not developing a real relationship with Christ at an early age made it easy to leave Christianity behind.

Later that same year when I first arrived I started school and made friends. As we got a little older, we started working and going out partying just about every weekend. It was a close knit group of three, with many other friends, but mainly the three of us would always hang out: myself, Marcel S. and Jorge C. At that time in our lives Jorge and I were not going to church, but Marcel was. In fact, he had to. No matter how late we got home on Saturday night, his mother made him go to church in the morning. It is a good thing we never drank or got into anything we should not have, otherwise, he would have had a much harder time on Sunday mornings.

So, every Saturday night on the way home, from wherever it was we were coming back from, Marcel would always ask this question; "so, who's coming to church with me tomorrow?" We would laugh at him and say, yeah we know, misery loves company. For some reason, he never got the message, and each time on the way home, he would ask the same question, "so, who's coming with me to church tomorrow?"

This went on for a couple years and sadly he never got us to go, until one night. As usual, he asked the question when we were all tired, and had no intention of getting up in the morning, period, never mind early in the morning. However, this night was different. On this night, there was no response to the question. It was silent, and for a brief moment nobody said a word. Then Jorge said, "I'll go with you tomorrow, man." I was taken aback and said to Jorge, "are you for real, you are going?" To which he replied, "yeah, I'll go."

You see from time to time we would prank each other, so it would have been perfectly normal for me to think Jorge was trying to prank me by making me get up in the morning and go to church tired while he stayed home and slept; but I just had a gut feeling this was not a prank, Jorge was really going to go. So then I said, "if you go, I'll go." So the next morning we all met up at Marcel's church. Back then it was called IBB, International Bible Baptist Church, in Miami; and for the next twenty years, we went to church together.

So much has happened to me over the years that I cannot even begin to speak, lest even believers would think I was making it up, but when God gets ready to take you for a ride, be ready to have your mind blown! Now some thirty years later, I still look back at that night as the night God decided it was time for me to get right with Him, and I am so glad I started down that path.

Acknowledgement:

I want to thank my beautiful wife, Ana, for her steady encouragement throughout our journey together. It has not always been an easy road, but I am forever grateful for her and for all the motivation she gives me in every endeavor.

I also want to thank my sister in Christ, Angie M. Had she not asked the question, as recorded in this book, it is highly unlikely I would have ever gotten around to committing this revelation to paper. Thank you, Angie, for the question and the extreme patience you exhibited as you waited for me to finish the book so that you could get a proper answer!

Lastly, I want to thank my two beautiful girls, Caitlyn and Mayah. Since birth, they have been nothing but a blessing to my wife and I. I cannot imagine two better behaved children who have grown into wonderful God fearing women. May our Father in heaven turn His face toward you, keep and protect you, continue to bless you both, and give you His everlasting peace!

Dedication:

This book is dedicated to two very important people in my life. First, I want to dedicate this book to my mother, Lorna. Obviously, without her, I would not be here. Yet, it is so much more than that. Without her continuous prayers, I certainly would not be here. Having a praying mother can make all the difference in the world, and it certainly has in my life. Discussing the scriptures with my mother, and learning so much from her about faith and trusting God in everything has been invaluable. I am so grateful for my mother; it is truly beyond words.

I also want to dedicate this book to my brother, Raymond. I do not believe I know a more selfless person than my brother, a man who would truly give you the very shirt off his back. When I look back at my childhood, one of the things that stand out is that my brother was always there for me, no matter what. Even today, I know I can always count on him. I cannot imagine what my life would be like had I not had my brother.

All my siblings, now four sisters, and myself, look up to him. When my kids were little, they would always say "Uncle Raymond should be President of The United States." That was always funny to me, because at their age, I could not have told you who was running the country, never mind nominating someone to do so.

Now they never wanted their uncle to be president just because he gave them gifts. It was because they realized he was just that great of a person, and as young as they were, even they could see it. Absolutely no one can claim to have a better brother than mine.

Revelations from Genesis
The Untold Biblical Story of Creation
Who Cain Feared and Where They Came From

Introduction:

It is never an easy thing to do, going against the grain. Sometimes falling in line and walking in the same direction as the masses is just less controversial. However, when you decide to live for the LORD, going against the societal, and sometimes, even religious grain is a must!

Living for the Father turns you into a societal contrarian, and once you accept that fact, life can become much clearer. I do not believe it is possible to live for God while, at the same time, conforming to society—unless the place where you live is truly Godly; if such a place even exists. As a societal contrarian you become more focused on what is important, your thoughts more in tuned, and you free yourself to worship the LORD as He commands; in spirit and in truth. It does not make you perfect, or more holy than thou, just a little more sensitive to the Spirit.

While many sometimes see contrarians simply as pot stirrers, the truth is, most simply just resist the ever daunting pressure to conform. Mostly to those things that are morally debased, yet even to those things that are simply biblically incorrect. Eventually, all the pressure to conform will fade, and nothing satisfies you more than knowing outside forces have little to no effect on you, and the only thing you want to conform to is the Word.

After God opened my eyes to the fact that we got the creation story wrong, it was not going to be hard for me to share. At least, so I thought. The problem I found was not the willingness to, but rather the knowing how to. After just one attempt it quickly became obvious to me that I had no idea how to explain it correctly never mind convincingly. Only now after writing this book do I feel my thoughts are more organized, and having something to refer people to most certainly helps.

For centuries we have understood that the Bible teaches us that God first created Adam then later determined that it was not good that he should be alone. After causing him to fall into a deep sleep, He removed one of his ribs and formed the first female, Eve, as she would later be named. Then after some time had passed, they had two sons. Sadly, when the sons grew, the eldest son slew his younger brother and was then exiled by God. He was sentenced to live the life of a fugitive and a vagabond as punishment; but for some seemingly unexplained reason, he became fearful of others that supposedly did not yet exist, finding and killing him.

What will surprise you is that for the most part, this is neither entirely true nor biblical. The biblical account actually says something different. In fact, the Bible says something very different. Yes, your Bible, which you have in your possession right now, says something very different from what you were taught, and even what you may believe you have read.

Sadly there is information from the book of Genesis about creation that has been skipped over and ignored or simply misunderstood; leading us to believe what we were taught without any further examination or study. Yet, if you ask someone to explain the Genesis account of the creation of man, and who it was Cain feared, they would have to resort to what I term as 'Bible Gymnastics' to try to explain the events that took place during and after creation.

Now, I define 'Bible Gymnastics' as having to bend, stretch, twist, turn and flip the scriptures to make it fit what we already believe. Many individuals even go as far as changing what the scriptures say to make it conform to their understanding, and then go on to share with others that same misinformation.

In the case of creation, because so much is completely missed or misunderstood, we forwent the true story and bought into what is tantamount to a fable. Hence the subject matter that this book covers, for instance. Who or what was it exactly that Cain feared once he was sentenced to be exiled from his home? If it was people, where did they, and his wife for that matter, come from?

The explanations given by some are interesting, but are they biblical? The explanations range from Cain being afraid of his nieces and nephews who wanted revenge for their father's murder; to Cain and Abel's siblings wanting revenge for the murder of their older brother. Additionally, it is explained that he may have been fearful of the future. Fearful siblings not yet born would learn of his guilt then find and kill him. Furthermore, they claim Cain's wife had to be either one of his sisters or possibly a niece.

Reading through you will find that all of these explanations are examples of Bible Gymnastics. Bending, stretching, twisting, turning, flipping and just plain making stuff up whole cloth in order to give answers to events not yet fully understood. However, making the Bible conform to what we believe just does not seem to be what our Father intended! Furthermore, the Bible has never needed to be interpreted as it is very capable of interpreting itself.

If the Bible is purposefully not clear on a particular matter, there may be room for intelligent conjecture. However, there must be a solid biblical basis for the conjecture, or it is just purely your personal opinion or the opinion of someone else from whom you adopted it. Not that having and sharing an opinion is necessarily a bad thing. Nonetheless, if we understood what the Bible taught, there would be less need for the filling in of 'gaps', because the 'gaps', for the most part—do not exist outside of our own lack of understanding.

Could Cain's fear of his nieces and nephews be feasible when the Bible does not say he even had any at the time his punishment was rendered? Would a fear of the unborn, to the point where he felt his punishment for murder was too great, be rational? Would it be reasonable to consider his wife to be a relative when, again, the scriptures do not say he had any, nor makes any inferences from which that can be drawn—other than the fact that he simply gained a wife?

The explanations given are all gap fillers. Trying to fill self-created gaps derived from our miss-understanding, due to a lack of studying, and maybe even an absence of curiosity. The question is, does the Bible tell us where Cain's wife came from? Does it tell us who or what it was Cain was in fear of finding and killing him? If it was indeed other people, then does the Bible tell us where those other people came from? The answer to each of these questions is a resounding yes! The Bible does tell us, and this book will help you to see those answers even though they are already conspicuously recorded in the scriptures.

When you are done reading this book, you will not only come to understand that it was in fact people that Cain feared, but you will also know where they came from, and when they first appeared. You will also understand where it was that Cain's wife came from.

In fact, in order to properly understand the story of creation we really only need to study our Bible. When we stop reading stories in the Bible as though we already know them and begin to read the Word prayerfully, having a hunger for new revelation, we will find God's Word will open up and reveal to us truths we have never seen before. It is my prayer that we all begin to study God's Word prayerfully with a desire to learn more, and get closer to our Father.

Revelations from Genesis
The Untold Biblical Story of Creation
Who Cain Feared and Where They Came From

Preface:

One afternoon after church service, a young lady named Angie M, a sister in Christ, asked the youth leader a question. The youth leader, taking over for the pastor that day, had just given a great teaching to the church on Gen. 6:3. However, her question was on a completely different subject altogether. Thinking back on it now, it was probably providence that she would ask this particular question, having nothing to do with the service that day, and me being there to hear it as it is the whole reason for me writing this book.

It was obvious that the question had been on her mind, and she really wanted an answer. She wanted to know who the people were that Cain feared when he told God his punishment was greater than he could bear, and where those people came from.

Now, as a side note, God had given me a revelation on Gen. 6:3 back in 1997, and I had never heard it preached before or since until the youth leader preached on it that day. Hearing that verse taught in 2022, and done so accurately for the first time, twenty five years after receiving the revelation was a pleasant surprise—to say the least. I would certainly recommend a study on Gen. 6:3. In fact, let me challenge you to do so, but be sure to pray and ask the Father for a clear understanding—so that you get the correct teaching, which is nothing short of incredible.

Getting back to my story; loving to talk about the Bible, I interjected myself into the conversation and attempted to answer her question, giving her the short version for the sake of time. However, when I had finished explaining, the look on her face said it all. Clearly, she did not agree with nor fully understand the short version of my response, and so her question remained unanswered.

Right then, I realized how much of an idiot I was. Although the Bible clearly tells us the, who, what, where, and when of creation, I failed to recognize the fact that we all have had such a skewed concept of the events of creation; that it has to be re-explained in detail. You have to first tackle the preconceived understanding most believers have, which may then open the door to understanding it correctly.

That, of course, is much easier said than done, because what the mass majority of people believe about creation is basically set in stone—so it cannot be easily corrected. Even when reading it for themselves in their own Bible, it remains a task for them to make the adjustment in their understanding. In thinking I could just give a quick synopsis of the reality of Cain's worries probably ranks up there with some of my most naive moments; of which there are many. Just saying how it was really was not saying much of anything at all without explaining it in detail. What the Bible actually says took place, as recorded by Moses, is an extremely far cry from what we are taught.

In other words, creation is so misunderstood, there is really no way of properly explaining it without first showing what has been missed. In order for people to even begin to understand what the Bible actually says about creation, and where the people Cain thought would pose a threat to him came from, you almost have to strip away everything that is currently understood.

Sadly, however, misunderstanding some of the simplicities of the scriptures is hardly anything new. There are quite a few verses and even whole stories in the Bible that have been misunderstood over the decades and even centuries.

Since we fail to study as we should, we accept the misunderstood versions that were handed down over the years as biblical truth, without questioning it. So, before we get into this revelation from the book of Genesis, we will take a look at a few examples of some commonly, and some not so commonly known scriptures that have been misunderstood.

Note, however, in looking at these examples of misunderstood scriptures and stories in the Bible; you must be aware that the understanding explained here is by no means all there is to know about a particular verse or story. As you may know, some verses have multiple meanings and so the exercise here is only to show what we got wrong. Not to show all that we should have gotten right, as that is clearly beyond my extremely limited knowledge.

Obviously, I would never claim to know it all and like everyone else I am constantly learning. In fact, I would not even claim to know any given percentage of the Bible. Not knowing what all it is we do not know makes it impossible to calculate the percentage we do know. All I know is that there is always more to learn, and I believe that is all we need to know. So let us take a look at some misunderstood verses.

Misunderstood Scriptures

You probably understood that God changed Saul's name to Paul after He met him on the road to Damascus. **He did not!**

You probably understood that the thief on the cross went to heaven with Christ, because He told the thief that he would be with Him in paradise the day they were crucified. **He did not!**

You also probably understood that the Bible tells us, as believers, that Jesus' return will be like a thief in the night. **It does not!**

Still, you probably understood that Noah's Ark took 120 years to build. **It did not!**

You also probably believed that Job was punished by God or that he was stripped of his blessings because of his self-righteousness, or at least because of something he did wrong. **He was not!**

In actuality, the reason for Job's suffering is incredibly profound. It is no surprise that Satan does not want us to fully understand what really took place! But we certainly will be going over it here.

I am pretty sure being taught and understanding these things to be true for many years you are probably thinking, 'this is insane; I have read these verses and these stories and I know them to be true.' Well, you may indeed know them to be true, but whether they are or not, we will have to let the Bible have the last word.

So like I said, these are but a few misunderstood scriptures and in some instances, they have much more meaning than you may think. However, because they were taught incorrectly or we simply misunderstood what we read, we missed the true understanding; some of which greatly impacts the message being conveyed.

Now, with the exception of the building of the ark and the story of Job, I chose these scriptures as examples because they can be cleared up without too much fanfare. In truth, however, I just took more time explaining the building of the ark, but that too can be quickly explained. So let us take a minute to go through them before we delve into the events of creation. Hopefully, this will help you to see what I mean when I say some scriptures are misunderstood. There are many more misunderstood scriptures, but as is the case with the story of Job, many of them are not so easily explained—at least not by me.

God did not change Saul's name to Paul

Revelations from Genesis
The Untold Biblical Story of Creation
Who Cain Feared and Where They Came From

God did not change Saul's name to Paul.

If you have been a believer for any length of time, you most certainly would have heard the statement made that God changed Saul's name to Paul—after his conversion on the road to Damascus. However, it can only be stated that God changed Saul's name but not shown, and for a good reason; because that event never happened. Therefore, it cannot be found in the scriptures.

In fact, some translations never even use the name Paul or even make reference to the fact that Saul's other name was Paul; they simply refer to him as Saul throughout the scriptures. The NKJV (New King James Version), however, is one of the translations that does use his other name Paul, but it is clear from the scriptures that the name change was not due to God giving Saul a new name.

Acts 13: 9 NKJV Then Saul, who also is called Paul, filled with the Holy Spirit, looked intently at him.

The scripture says, "Saul who is <u>also</u> called Paul," not 'Saul who was later named Paul.' The truth is Paul was his Roman name, and Saul's was his Hebrew name. Now the following statement may very well be conjecture but conjecture based on a solid basis. It is reasonable to believe Saul may have started to use his Roman name, Paul, to distance himself from his reputation as Saul. Again, that is conjecture, but whether or not that was truly the case, however, it is clear from the scriptures that God did not change Saul's name to Paul. It was already his given name.

is did not tell the thief on the cross he would be
n Him in heaven that day meaning the day they

Revelations from Genesis
The Untold Biblical Story of Creation
Who Cain Feared and Where They Came From

Jesus did not tell the thief on the cross he would be with Him in heaven that day, meaning the day they were crucified.

First, it is important to note the original Hebrew and Aramaic manuscripts of the Old Testament were composed not only without vowels but also without punctuations or diacritical marks. As you will see, this fact will aid in explaining the misunderstanding of the statement Jesus made to the thief on the cross. More importantly, the correct understanding is backed up by other verses, which we will take a look at first. So as we read it in Luke 23, it says the following:

Luke 23: 42-43 KJV And he said onto Jesus, Lord, remember me when thou comest into thy kingdom. And Jesus said unto him, verily I say unto thee, to day shalt thou be with Me in paradise.

Luke 23:42-43 NKJV Then he said unto Jesus, Lord, remember me when you come into your kingdom. And Jesus said to him, assuredly, I say unto you, today you will be with Me in paradise.

Well, we know from other scriptures that Jesus did not go to paradise that day. We know he went to preach to the spirits of those imprisoned since the days of Noah.

1 Peter 3:19-20 NKJV by whom also he went and preached unto the spirits in prison; 20 who formerly were disobedient, when once the Devine longsuffering waited in the days of Noah, while the ark was being prepared, in which a few, that is, eight souls were saved through water.

1 Peter 3:19-20 KJV By which also he went and preached unto the spirits in prison; 20 Which sometime were disobedient, when once the longsuffering of God waited in the days of Noah, while the ark was a preparing, wherein few, that is, eight souls were saved by water.

Even more germane to this point, we also know that after His resurrection, three days after his death, He told Mary not to touch Him because He had not yet ascended to the Father.

John 20:17 KJV Jesus saith unto her, Touch me not; for I am not yet ascended to my Father: but go to my brethren, and say unto them, I ascend unto my Father, and your Father; and to my God, and your God.

John 20:17 NKJV Jesus said to her, "Do not cling to Me, for I have not yet ascended to My Father; but go to My brethren and say to them, 'I am ascending to My Father and your Father, and to My God and your God.' "

So clearly, Jesus had not yet gone to paradise and certainly not the day He was crucified; so then neither did the thief on the cross go to paradise that day. I would contend that the thief has yet to go to paradise, but the point here is that Jesus could not have meant the thief was going to be with Him in paradise that very day, knowing He would not yet be leaving.

So then what did Jesus mean by that statement? Well, to understand this verse is to be aware of the fact that the punctuations were not applied at the time the writing was recorded but sometime later during the translation. By simply putting the comma in the correct place, which is after the word 'today' and not before; then this verse lines up with the rest of the scriptures which tells us Christ did not go straight to heaven on the day He was crucified. Correctly understood, the statement Jesus made was the following:

Luke 23:43 NKJV And Jesus said to him, assuredly, I say unto you today, you will be with Me in paradise.

It was a statement of fact that Jesus was making on that day at that time. Jesus did not say the thief would be with Him in paradise that day, but on that day, He told the thief he would be with Him in paradise. At the same time, it must be noted that Jesus typically started a statement saying, 'Verily I say on to you' followed by the rest of His statement; which would have lead the translators to believe the comma belonged before the word 'today'.

Yet, even if we did not have the other verses that help to clear that up, we know that with the LORD, a day is a thousand years and a thousand years is but a day. This is God's way of saying the day never changes because time does not exist for Him. He is the same yesterday, today, and forever because it is all the same day. For God, yesterday, today and forever are right now. So when Jesus told the thief on the cross that he would be with Him in heaven on that day, where you put the comma then, really does not matter in terms of accuracy; because to God that day is today, and will be tomorrow.

Now, on the day of the LORD, when all those who have accepted Jesus as their LORD and Savior have died and are risen; so too will the thief who accepted Christ while on the cross. Then those who are alive at that time will be caught up in the air with them. The thief on the cross was not given a special invitation that allowed him to enter before anyone else.

Only two people recorded in the scriptures where taken to heaven and that would be Enoch and Elijah. There is an argument to be made for Moses but that requires more research. Two of the three never died and will return, but that is for another discussion. Certainly the thief on the cross, however, was not the fourth.

It is commonly understood that those who have died in Christ are currently in Heaven and will return on the day of the LORD. Then, those who are alive will be caught up with them in the air, and our bodies transformed in the twinkling of an eye. We have all heard this saying in reference to those believers who have passed; 'he/she is with the LORD now.' That is a claim that many make, but is that what the scriptures say?

The Bible teaches that the dead shall rise first, and then those who are alive will be caught up with them in the air. Now some say the dead that will rise are just the bodies of the dead believers and they will be rejoined with their souls, which are already in heaven, then their bodies changed into glorified, incorruptible bodies. Now that may sound plausible to some, but again is that what the Bible says? Well no, it does not say the bodies of the dead shall rise first. It says the dead shall rise first, referring to the believers who have died.

So, since the dead believers will rise first, from where will they rise? Up from heaven? Does that even make sense? Certainly not! The dead shall rise out of the earth and out of the water. If those who have died are already in heaven, then what need would there be for the dead to rise?

Back in the early days of the church there was concern by the believers in Thessalonica that their loved ones who had believed but died would not enter into heaven since they died before Jesus' return. They were saddened, because they thought there was no hope for their departed loved ones who would, supposedly, be forever separated from them, and from the Father.

However, had the dead already been in heaven, Paul could have easily cleared that up. All he had to do was make the same claim that some make today, and let it be known that their loved ones were already in heaven with the LORD. Yet, that is not at all what Paul did.

What Paul made clear to them was that those who are alive, at the time of Christ's return would not precede those who had died. Now why would Paul need to make that statement? Again, if the dead were already in heaven, why would Paul tell us, in no uncertain terms, that the living would not precede the dead? Why not just say something along the lines of; 'sorrow not for the dead because you believe they will not enter into heaven; rather rejoice because they have already gone to be with the LORD.' I mean, that is basically what we say today, is it not!

Pay close attention to what Paul actually said.

I Thess 4:13-18 NKJV But I do not want you to be ignorant, brethren, concerning those who have fallen asleep, lest you sorrow as others who have no hope. 14 For if we believe that Jesus died and rose again, even so God will bring with Him those who sleep in Jesus. 15 For this we say to you by the word of the Lord, that we who are alive and remain until the coming of the Lord will by no means precede those who are asleep. ¹⁶ For the Lord Himself will descend from heaven with a shout, with the voice of an archangel, and with the trumpet of God. And the dead in Christ will rise first. 17 Then we who are alive and remain shall be caught up together with them in the clouds to meet the Lord in the air. And thus we shall always be with the Lord. 18 Therefore comfort one another with these words.

Just in case you missed it let us take a look at verse 18 again.

"Therefore comfort one another with <u>these</u> words."

Paul said, concerning the dead, we are to comfort one another with 'these' words. Do those words you just read say the believers who have fallen asleep are already in heaven? No, not at all, In fact, they say the complete opposite. Paul clearly tells us the dead are not in heaven but will be risen on the day of the LORD and go up before those who remain alive. Then those who remain will be caught up with them in the air.

For whatever reason, in an attempt to comfort people who have lost loved ones we simply ignored Paul's words and made up our own, making entry into heaven an immediate affair. So now to justify our words we have to interpret the scriptures in ways to fit our beliefs.

We read verses like: 2 Cor 5:8 *KJV [We are confident, I say, and willing rather to be absent from the body, and to be present with the Lord.]* then declare that this means the moment we die we go straight to heaven, therefore, believers who have passed are in heaven right now.

Interestingly, however, there is actually some truth to people going home instantly in a sense, but not as understood, and we will come right back to this.

Furthermore, some refer to 1 Thess 4:14 as Paul stating that God will bring those who have fallen asleep with Him, on the day of the LORD, so they must already be in heaven if God will bring them with Him. However, that is not what Paul said. Let us read the verse again.

I Thess 4:14 KJV For if we believe that Jesus died and rose again, even so them also which sleep in Jesus will God bring with Him.

Paul is not saying that God will bring those who have died out from heaven back to earth with (God) on the LORD's day. What he is saying is that, just as God raised Jesus from the dead and brought Him to heaven so will He bring those believers who have died in Jesus with Jesus to Heaven.

The 'Him' in this verse is Jesus not God. Now, for the record, we know they are one in the same so let us not get turned around here. The point is, the believers who have placed their faith in Christ are at rest and will rise again on the LORD's day, not before.

As far as believers going home instantly we need to understand that from the time a believer dies to the time they will be raised from death no time will have passed—at least not for them, because time ceases to exist the moment we die. So, for the believer who dies, the rapture will occur the moment they die. For us it has yet to come and both things are not mutually exclusive, because for those who remain, we are still confined by the restraints of time, whereas the dead know no time.

...he Bible does not teach believers Jesus' return wil...
...like a thief in the night...

Revelations from Genesis
The Untold Biblical Story of Creation
Who Cain Feared and Where They Came From

The Bible does not teach believers Jesus' return will be like a thief in the night.

1Thess 5:2-3 NKJV For you yourselves know perfectly that the day of the LORD so comes as a thief in the night. 3 For when they shall say, peace and safety: then sudden destruction comes upon them, as labor pains upon a pregnant woman; and they shall not escape.

2 Peter 3:10 NKJV But the day of the LORD will come as a thief in the night, in which the heavens will pass away with a great noise, and the elements will melt with fervent heat; both the earth and the works that are in it will be burned up.

In one sense, it is pretty easy to see why these verses are understood the way they are. I mean, it clearly says, "the day of the LORD will come as a thief in the night", and so it will for many. Only it will not be so for believers.

In their respective letters, both Peter and Paul are referring to those who are unsaved, those who live in darkness. To them, Jesus' return will be like a thief in the night because they do not believe in Jesus, never mind the fact that He is coming back, but we, as believers, do. Just read the next verse.

1Thess 5:2-4 KJV But ye, brethren, are not in darkness, that that day should overtake you as a thief. 5 Ye are all children of light, and the children of the day; we are not of the night, nor of darkness. 6 Therefore let us not sleep, as do others; but let us watch and be sober.

The Hebrew word here for 'Darkness' σκότος / Skotos [SBLB - G4655] (of darkened eyesight or blindness. Metaphorically –of ignorance respecting Devine things and human duties, and the accompanying ungodliness and immorality, together with their consequent misery in hell).

So clearly, Jesus' return will be as a thief in the night to those who live in darkness, the unbelievers who are ignorant and blind to the divine things of God. However, to those that live in the light, we who see, the believers, it will not be so. Jesus' return should not come as a complete and total surprise to us. We should not only be praying for His return but be expecting it.

Noah's Ark did not take 120 years to build

Revelations from Genesis
The Untold Biblical Story of Creation
Who Cain Feared and Where They Came From

Noah's Ark did not take 120 years to build.

The notion that the ark was built in one hundred and twenty years, was basically derived from people misunderstanding Gen 6:3.

Gen 6:3 KJV And the LORD said, My spirit shall not always strive with man, for that he also is flesh: yet his days shall be an hundred and twenty years.

Gen 6:3 NKJV And the LORD said, "My Spirit shall not strive with man forever, for he is indeed flesh; yet his days shall be one hundred and twenty years."

(Remember, this is the verse of which I spoke of at the beginning, wherein I challenged you to prayerfully study it). From this verse, it has been understood that the ark took one hundred and twenty years to build as God patiently waited for mankind to repent. However, in reality this verse has nothing to do with God's decision to bring a flood.

While God did indeed patiently wait many years, giving mankind the opportunity to repent during the construction of the ark, it was not for a period of one hundred and twenty years. The one hundred and twenty years in Gen 6:3 has two meanings that I have found thus far, but neither has anything to do with the ark.

One is the maximum length of time on earth for each individual person after the flood, albeit not immediately after the flood, and the other is what I challenged you to study for yourself.

However, God did not bring the flood to wipe mankind and beast off the earth because of how He made us. We had no choice in how we were made. The reason God brought the flood is found in Gen 6:5-6

Gen 6:5-6 KJV And GOD saw that the wickedness of man was great in the earth, and that every imagination of the thoughts of his heart was only evil continually. 6 And it repented the LORD that he had made man on the earth, and it grieved him at his heart.

Notice again in Gen 6:3 God said he would not always strive with man because of how He made us [flesh – meaning corruptible]; but here in Gen 6:5-6 Moses tells us God was grieved at His heart because of what we had become, (wicked), thinking only evil thoughts, thus doing evil deeds, continually. That, indeed, was a choice we made.

So then Gen 6:3 and Gen 6:5-6 are showing us two completely separate issues God was addressing. On the one hand was the issue of how we were made. On the other was the issue of what we had become.

Therefore, the setting of the one hundred and twenty years by God was not in response to man's behavior but rather a response to man's condition. In response to man's behavior, because it grieved God that He had made mankind, He decided to destroy them from off the face of the earth. He told Noah the end of all flesh was before Him because of what we had become, (wicked, evil, violent), not because of how we were made.

Gen 6:13 KJV And God said to Noah, "the end of all flesh is come before Me for the earth is filled with violence through them; and behold, I will destroy them with the earth."

Gen 6:13 NKJV And God said to Noah, "The end of all flesh has come before Me, for the earth is filled with violence through them; and behold, I will destroy them with the earth."

Since mankind did not retain God in their hearts or minds, but rather gave themselves over to a reprobate mind only contemplating evil deeds—God decided to erase them and start anew.

Now, as I stated, the Ark was not built in one hundred and twenty years, as is understood. It was actually built in less than ninety six years, and to see this, we simply need to read the scriptures as written. Note, however, I am not saying the ark was built in 'x' amount of years; only that it was not built in one hundred and twenty, and certainly less than ninety six; as recorded by Moses.

Now, the Bible states, Noah was five hundred years old when He begat Shem, Ham, and Japheth.

Gen 5:32 NKJV And Noah was five hundred years old and begot Shem, Ham and Japheth.

When studied, we find they were not triplets; neither were they recorded in that verse in order of birth. In fact, for some reason they were mentioned completely out of order. In that Noah was five hundred years old when he had his first son Japheth, who is mentioned last. He is five hundred and three when he had his second son Shem, who is mentioned first; then Ham, his third son, who is mentioned second.

I have not been able to determine Noah's exact age when he had Ham, but he was certainly born sometime shortly after Shem. So we know from the scriptures that God spoke to Noah, telling him to build the Ark when he had his three sons, meaning he was over five hundred years old. Yet he was six hundred years old when he entered the completed ark, and God shut the door and brought the flood.

Gen 7:6-7 NKJV Now, Noah was six hundred years old when the floodwaters were on the earth. So Noah, with his sons, his wife, and his sons' wives, went into the ark, because of the waters of the flood.

So if Noah was over five hundred years old when God instructed him to build the ark and he was six hundred when he entered, it clearly shows us the Ark was built in less than one hundred years. There is an argument to be made from these scriptures that it could be less than ninety five years of building the ark since Noah had all three sons before getting the command from God to build it. So if Ham was just two years younger than Shem, it would be under ninety five years of construction; but we will stay with under ninety six years to be sure.

Now seeing that Noah was over five hundred when he got the command, and six hundred when he entered the finished ark, it is hard to understand how that got so confused since it is pretty clear. Sadly, however, in a poor attempt to compensate for the discrepancy of time, I heard it said on one occasion, that Noah had his three sons when he was four hundred and eighty years old. Now if that were the case, you would also have to make Noah's sons triplets for it to work. This is yet another classic case of Bible gymnastics.

The Bible says Shem, Noah's second born, had his first born, Arphaxad, when he was one hundred years old, and that was two years after the flood.

Gen 11:10 NKJV This is the genealogy of Shem: Shem was one hundred years old and begot Arphaxed two years after the flood.

We know from Gen 8:13 that Noah was six hundred and one years old after the flood.

Gen 8:13 NKJV And it came to pass in the six hundredth, and first year, in the first month, the first day of the month, the waters were dried up from off the face of the earth...

So if Arphaxad was born two years after the flood and Shem was one hundred years old when he had him, then that would mean Noah was six hundred and three years old when Arphaxad was born. This, in turn, means Noah had to have begotten Shem when he was five hundred and three.

Now since Noah begat Shem when he was five hundred and three years old and was instructed to build the ark after all his sons were born, then he entered the ark when he was six hundred years old; then clearly the ark was built in under 97 years. When you account for the fact that Ham was born after Shem and before Noah received the instructions to build the ark, then at the least you would have to deduct one more year and that would be at a minimum.

Therefore, if Ham was born just a year after Shem that would put the start time for the building of the ark at the very earliest, when Noah was five hundred and four years old. Whether or not his sons were also married before God spoke to Noah or God simply mentioned Noah's son's wives because they would be married by the time the ark was completed is up for debate. At least, it's not so clear to me at this time.

However, understanding the ark was not built in one hundred and twenty years is the correct understanding.

Job was not being punished by God

Revelations from Genesis
The Untold Biblical Story of Creation
Who Cain Feared and Where They Came From

Job was not being punished by God.

Some have considered the story of Job to be a parable. However, the events leading up to Job's tribulation, and the events of the story itself make it very clear that Job was indeed a real person. Had the story of Job been a parable, we would not have gotten so much detail about Job's life, character, and personhood.

God makes it a point of expressing His acknowledgement and approval of Job's qualities and that is just not something found when discussing fictitious characters. Furthermore, once you understand what the story of Job really represents, you will see it could only be played out by a real event.

Lastly, the Bible could not fictitiously state that Satan made such a damming accusation against God, and use a made up character to prove Satan wrong. The nature of the accusation required it be answered by man—a real living being. What accusation, you ask? Well, we will get into it very shortly.

Still, those who understand the story of Job to be real have misunderstood the events of his story. They concluded that God was punishing Job mainly because of his purported 'self-righteousness' or some other character flaw or sin in his life. However, that could not be further from the truth.

In fact, if it were not for Job's steadfast faith in, obedience to, fear of, and love for God, we probably would not be here today; or at least not living life as we currently experience it. That may sound like hyperbole, but I can assure you it most certainly is not. So let me explain.

Now, the story of Job really starts in heaven. Satan, although having been thrown out of heaven, is allowed to enter. Possibly because he is required to give an account to the Father for his day to day activities.

Job 1:6-7 NKJV Now there was a day when the sons of God came to present themselves before the LORD, and Satan also came among them. 7 And the LORD said to Satan, "From where do you come?" So Satan answered the LORD and said, "From going to and fro on the earth, and from walking back and forth on it."

Satan comes in with the angels, and God calls him out, asking where he was. He has no trouble telling God where he was, but is sure to avoid telling God what he was actually doing. He calmly states he had been walking up and down the earth, but God, obviously knowing exactly what he was up to, then asks him if he had considered His servant Job.

Job 1:8 NKJV Then the LORD said to Satan, "Have you considered My servant Job that there is none like him on the earth, a blameless and upright man, one who fears God and shuns evil?

Satan quickly drops the act, then, in an end-around way admits he had indeed considered Job, but had been unable to harm him nor anything belonging to him. He then accuses Job of only serving God for the benefits and the favor he receives from God, but not because he loves Him. In front of heaven and all the angels, in essence, Satan was accusing God of having to buy man's love and obedience.

Job 1:9-11 NKJV So Satan answered the LORD and said, "Does Job fear God for nothing? 10 Have You not made a hedge around him, around his household, and around all that he has on every side? You have blessed the work of his hands, and his possessions have increased in the land. 11 But now, stretch out Your hand and touch all that he has, and he will surely curse You to Your face!"

Satan's accusation reached far beyond Job. He was making the claim that mankind, as a whole, only served God because of what He did for them. If God were to stop helping, protecting, and blessing mankind, they would surely turn on Him. Even curse Him to His face. Without hesitation, God tells Satan to go prove his claim.

*Job 1:12 NKJV And the L*ORD *said to Satan, "Behold, all that he has is in your power; only do not lay a hand on his person."*

Satan was more than happy to take on the challenge and prove his claim to be true. He would now get what he wanted all along. To show that God was a fraud, claiming mankind was faithful and obedient to Him, because they loved Him. He was so elated he wasted no time in plotting and planning his attack on poor Job. To ensure he got the results he wanted he held no punches; with the exception of the one thing he was not allowed to do, which was physically harming Job.

What would have happened to humanity had Job failed this test, and Satan's accusations were proven to be true?

So after much scheming Satan devised the perfect collapse of Job's empire. His plan had to be so ruthless that it could only achieve his desired outcome; Job's rejection of God. Satan went after everything near and dear to Job, his family and his possessions. Satan literally wrought hell on earth for Job.

Job 1: NKJV13-19 Now there was a day when his sons and daughters were eating and drinking wine in their oldest brother's house; 14 and a messenger came to Job and said, "The oxen were plowing and the donkeys feeding beside them, 15 when the Sabeans raided them and took them away - indeed they have killed the servants with the edge of the sword; and I alone have escaped to tell you!" 16 While he was still speaking, another also came and said, "The fire of God fell from heaven and burned up the sheep and the servants, and consumed them; and I alone have escaped to tell you!"

17 While he was still speaking, another also came and said, "The Chaldeans formed three bands, raided the camels and took them away, yes, and killed the servants with the edge of the sword; and I alone have escaped to tell you!" 18 While he was still speaking, another also came and said, "Your sons and daughters were eating and drinking wine in their oldest brother's house, 19 and suddenly a great wind came from across the wilderness and struck the four corners of the house, and it fell on the young people, and they are dead; and I alone have escaped to tell you!"

Now, we have all had our bad days and unfortunately, will continue to have them, but what happened to Job was beyond unbelievably unbearable for most. Satan had taken Job to the limits then took him a step beyond. Whatever Satan thought of that would sever, destroy, obliterate even annihilate Job's relationship to the Father that is what he did. Satan was sure he won, having taken everything from Job, leaving him with nothing, not even hope; or so he thought. With glee, Satan stood by and waited for the words to leave Job's mouth as Job stood up to speak. Surely I broke him, Satan must have thought to himself, but Job had something different to say.

Job 1:20 NKJV Then Job arose, tore his robe, and shaved his head; and he fell to the ground and worshiped. 21 And he said: "Naked I came from my mother's womb, And naked shall I return there. The LORD gave, and the LORD has taken away; Blessed be the name of the LORD."22 In all this Job did not sin nor charge God with wrong.

What a blow this must have been to Satan. He was so sure Job would have done exactly as expected. However, Job, in the face of absolute horror, profound sadness, and utter despair, instead of cursing God worships Him, and declares His sovereignty. Certainly, this is not the reaction of a self-righteous person. Job was exactly who God said he was, blameless and upright, and one who feared God and shunned evil.

Satan had to eat crow and be put in his place once again, and must have dreaded having to come back before the LORD having so shamefully been proven wrong. Returning to heaven, again to give an account of his time, head hung low, the scene played out once again. However, it appears Satan had a moment where the proverbial light-bulb went off in his head, and he thought he had what was the answer to why his plan failed. In not so many words he declares he was tricked by God not been allowed to fully bring Job to his knees, and had he been allowed to Job would have surely cursed God.

Job 2: 1-5 NKJV Again there was a day when the sons of God came to present themselves before the LORD, and Satan came also among them to present himself before the LORD.2 And the LORD said to Satan, "From where do you come?" Satan answered the LORD and said, "From going to and fro on the earth, and from walking back and forth on it." 3 Then the LORD said to

Satan, "Have you considered My servant Job, that there is none like him on the earth, a blameless and upright man, one who fears God and shuns evil? And still he holds fast to his integrity, ..."4 So Satan answered the LORD and said, "Skin for skin! Yes, all that a man has he will give for his life. 5 But stretch out Your hand now, and touch his bone and his flesh, and he will surely curse You to Your face!"

Satan was sure he had pin pointed the root cause of his failure. He was tricked by God and set up to fail. Surely God would not let him physically harm Job since that was the key to Job holding on to his faith. God, however, wasted no time and said, he is in your hands; only you cannot kill him.

Job 2:6 NKJV And the LORD said to Satan, "Behold, he is in your hand, but spare his life."

Satan turned and set out to finish the job he started while the iron was still hot. After striking Job with painful boils all over his body, making it hard for Job to walk or sit without pain, never giving him rest from his suffering; he put the very words he wanted Job to say in his wife's mouth so she could spoon feed it to him. He wanted to make sure Job felt his reward for worshipping God in the midst of his worst fears was simply more punishment.

Job 2:7-9 NKJV So Satan went out from the presence of the LORD, and struck Job with painful boils from the sole of his foot to the crown of his head. 8 And he took for himself a potsherd with which to scrape himself while he sat in the midst of the ashes. 9 Then his wife said to him, "Do you still hold fast to your integrity? Curse God and die!"

To this day it is believed that Job had some level of blame, and so God allowed him to be punished. The truth is Job was blameless, so God allowed him to stand up on behalf of us all. Job was not punished by God, nor did he have fault. Because of Job's faith and obedience he was able to withstand the onslaught even though he felt like he was being unjustly punished. He had no idea he was standing up against the accusation of the Devil for the sake of mankind. With all the torment, Job did not turn his back on God. He wanted answers, yes, but although all he received from God was favor throughout his years—when the bad times were upon him; he held on to the fact that even in those times, he could still trust God.

Job 2:10 NKJV But he said to her, "You speak as one of the foolish women speaks. Shall we indeed accept good from God, and shall we not accept adversity?" In all this, Job did not sin with his lips.

Satan was not done with Job. He had one last shot at getting Job to turn against God. While he suffered in pain, depression, and deep sorrow, Satan turned to Job's friends to condemn him; attempting to push him ever deeper into the abyss. It is extremely important to note, however, that it was not just Job's three friends that condemned Job; but a fourth person shows up to further antagonize Job. I believe the misunderstanding of the actions of this fourth person, and not seeing how God dealt with him, has caused the continued condemnation of Job to this day.

Now Job's three friends show up to comfort and mourn with him. However, Job's condition was so dreadful, not only was it hard to recognize him, it gave the impression that he was surely being punished by God. All they could do was sit with him and say nothing. Day after day, night after night, they came out and sat with Job, but for seven days no one said a word.

Certainly what they must have thought was, what great sin did Job commit that caused God to unleash such wrath on him. However, to their dismay, when Job finally speaks, he does not admit to his sin but rather curses the day he was born, and declares he knows not why God was punishing him. His friends who came to mourn with him, and comfort him, who could not say a word because of the level of despair and pain they saw him in could not believe the audacity of Job. They could not believe that in his state Job was basically declaring his innocence. They were there to counsel Job, using words of wisdom and comfort, but instead, they could only find words of chastisement in the spirit of condemnation.

Back and forth they went, each taking their turn attempting to get Job to acknowledge his sin. Not knowing what God was doing, nor fully understanding that God causes it to rain on the just as well as the unjust. They were left condemning Job for not admitting fault, which to them meant Job was claiming God was unjust. Lastly, this fourth person comes into the picture. One younger than Job and his friends, and this person has a very interesting name. His name is Elihu, which translated means, [God Himself] SAC.

Elihu then proceeds to explain the reason for his silence and why he must now step in, but also expresses his distain towards all four of them—Job and his three friends. He was upset with Job because in his eyes he perceived Job was being self-righteous and acting indignant. He was also upset with Job's friends because they failed to correct Job. They allowed him to repel their statements and squirm out of every corner. Elihu then expresses to Job that he comes to him in place of God.

Job 33:6 KJV Behold, I am according to thy wish in God's stead:...

The problem is, Elihu was not God and did not represent nor speak for God. This is where so many have gotten the story of Job confused. God decided it was time to put an end to Job's suffering so He stepped in and vindicated Job; but at the same time He let Job know that God does not have to give an explanation for His actions to anyone. The problem is, when God steps in, it is widely believed that God immediately addressed Job, but that is not so. God steps in, and immediately addresses Elihu, the one who claimed to speak on God's behalf. The Bible states the following that is basically misunderstood, which is why so many believe God jumped on Job:

Job 38:1NKJV Then the LORD answered Job out of the whirlwind, and said...

Now, it has to be noted that Eliphaz chided Job, telling him to call out to God, because he thought Job was being self-righteous; having refused to admit to his sin that had lead to his destruction.

Eliphaz said to Job: "Call out now; is there anyone who will answer you?" Job 5:1 NKJV

Twice Job cried out for God to answer him.

Job 30:20 NKJV "I cry out to You, but You do not answer me;

Job 31:35 NKJV ...Oh, that the Almighty would answer me,...

Job wanted God to tell him what he did wrong or vindicate him. So now, when God showed up, it was an answer to Job's cry, hence the statement: *Then the LORD answered Job out of the whirlwind, and said...*

It was not that in answering Job he was initially speaking directly to him, and in fact, He was not.

Two other things should be considered when trying to understand who it was God first spoke to. The first is, who was speaking the moment God stepped in? Second, who was there with Job, and for what purpose? Both of these considerations are important because of the very first question, albeit rhetorical, that God asked when He showed up.

So, to answer the first question, who was speaking? The answer is Elihu. Elihu was the one speaking when he is actually cut off by God showing up in a whirlwind. To answer the second question, who was there with job and for what purpose? The answer is, Job's three friends were there, along with Elihu who just shows up, and they were there to mourn and comfort Job. However, in their minds, because of Job's failure to admit he sinned, it turned into a counseling slash condemning sessions. So now God's first question was this:

Job 38:2 NKJV Who is this who darkens counsel by words without knowledge?

You need to understand that Job was the one being counseled; he was not counseling his three friends. All three of Job's friends were guilty of darkening counsel without wisdom, but Elihu's guilt was most egregious. In fact, this question that God posed to Elihu was addressing the very thing Elihu twice accused Job of doing.

Elihu stated: "Therefore Job opens his mouth in vain; He multiplies words without knowledge." Job 35:6 NKJV

"Job hath spoken without knowledge, and his words were without wisdom." Job 34:35 NKJV

So now God accuses Elihu of speaking words without knowledge and asks, "who is this who darkens counsel by words without knowledge?" *Job 38:2 NKJV*

Amongst other things, Elihu claimed his lips utter pure knowledge;

Job 33:3 NKJV My words come from my upright heart; My lips utter pure knowledge.

He also professed to be speaking on God's behalf only he claimed to be less terrifying than God.

Job 33: 6 KJV Behold, I am according to thy wish in God's stead: I also am formed out of the clay. 7 Behold, my terror shall not make thee afraid, neither shall my hand be heavy upon thee.

Then, in the most egregious act, Elihu basically declares to Job that he is on par with God.

Job 36:4 NKJ For truly my words shall not be false: he that is perfect in knowledge is with thee.

With all the boasting of his perfect knowledge it is no wonder the first thing God did was put Elihu in his place. In his arrogance, Elihu had challenged Job to do to him what he did to his three friends.

Job 33:5 NKJV If you can answer me, Set your words in order before me; Take your stand.

The Hebrew word for 'answer' here is (שׁוּב 'shub') SAC [to turn back]. So Elihu was challenging Job to repel him, if he could, like Job did to his three friends.

Elihu then accuses Job of thinking too highly of himself, which in fact was exactly what Elihu was doing. He also accused Job of keeping company with wicked men, claiming Job said there is no gain in serving God. In other words, Job too was wicked.

Job 34:7-9 NKJV What man is like Job, Who drinks scorn like water, 8 Who goes in company with the workers of iniquity, And walks with wicked men? 9 For he has said, "It profits a man nothing that he should delight in God."

That is not at all what Job said, however. What Job said was that the wicked say it does not profit a man to serve God. Job brings up the wicked in Job 21:7 and then mentions the statement about it not profiting a man anything as what the wicked say in Job 21:15. Not that it is what Job believes.

Job stated: *"Why do the wicked live and become old, Yes, become mighty in power?"Job 21:7 NKJV*

"Yet <u>they</u> say to God, 'Depart from us, For we do not desire the knowledge of Your ways. 15 Who is the Almighty, that we should serve Him? And what profit do we have if we pray to Him?" Job 21:14-15 NKJV

Not only was Job stating that it was the saying of the wicked, he even separated himself from them in the same statement.

Job 21:16 NKJV Indeed their prosperity is not in their hand; The counsel of the wicked is far from me.

Still, Elihu, in his arrogance and anger sought to ascribe that saying to Job. Now, Elihu was very angry with both Job and his friends, but he attempted to hide his true feelings by telling Job he really only desired to justify him, even while Elihu displayed his arrogance and contempt.

Job 33:31-33 KJV Mark well, O Job, hearken unto me: hold thy peace, and I will speak. 32 If thou hast anything to say, answer me: speak, for I desire to justify thee. 33 If not, hearken unto me: hold thy peace, and I shall teach thee wisdom.

That truly was a dishonest and arrogant statement by Elihu, because his whole point was that Job was self-righteous, and his friends incapable of getting him to confess his sin. Elihu's sole purpose was to condemn Job because his friends failed to do so. Now in a dishonest and deceptive move he claimed he wanted to justify Job. However, it didn't take long for Elihu to contradict himself and once again expose his true intentions, as he then said his desire it that Job be tried unto the end.

Job 34:35 NKJV My desire is that Job may be tried unto the end because of his answers for wicked men.

It cannot be both. He cannot have the desire to justify Job and at the same time have the desire that he be tried unto the end. Elihu was trying hard to cloak his distain towards Job, and he was going to be the one to break him and get him to openly acknowledge his sin.

Now when God showed up, He proceeded to excoriate Elihu, making it clear he did not speak on God's behalf nor was he perfect in knowledge. Just as Elihu told Job to answer him, God now tells Elihu he must answer God.

Job 38:3 NKJV Now prepare yourself like a man; I will question you, and you shall answer Me.

Job 38:3 KJV Gird up now thy loins like a man; for I will demand of thee, and answer thou Me.

The Hebrew word for 'answer' in this verse is (עֲדֵי 'yada') SAC [to make known]. This is different from the word Elihu used when speaking to Job. So God told Elihu, now I will ask the questions, and you make known to me, you teach me. Then God proceeded to grill Elihu with question his perfect knowledge and pure wisdom had no answers for.

Once God was finished with Elihu, He then turned to Job and told him he too must now prepare himself like a man, and answer to God.

Job 40:7 NKJV Now prepare yourself like a man; I will question you, and you shall answer Me:

Job 40:7 KJV Gird up thy loins now like a man: I will demand of thee, and declare thou unto Me.

Oddly enough, those who missed the fact that God first addressed Elihu with this statement just assumed God stated it to Job twice which really makes no sense. Now, Job's reply is very telling. Job goes back to God's initial rhetorical question addressed to Elihu, and brings it around to himself.

Job 42:3 KJV Who is he that hideth counsel without knowledge? Therefore have I uttered that I understood not.

Now, why would Job do that? Why would he, after seeing God just annihilate Elihu, put himself under that same spotlight? Simple really, you see it does not matter who you are or whether you are right or wrong. When God shows up, all you see is how small and insignificant you are. No matter what the argument, being right no longer matters. All of a sudden, you come to the realization that what you know about God amounts to nothing, and what you are in disagreement over means nothing. All your troubles quietly steal away, and all that is left is you and God. What a humbling experience it must have been.

In humility, Job acknowledges he too knew nothing about God, even though what he said was right and what all others said was wrong. When God was done correcting Job, letting him know He does not need to explain what He is doing to anyone, nor does He need to explain what Job did wrong or vindicate him; he then turns to Eliphaz. He tells him that He is angry with him and his two friends because they did not speak what is right about God like Job had.

Notice God makes the statement that they had not spoken what was right as Job did twice, which is notable. God instructed them to take sacrifices and go to Job then he will pray for forgiveness for them. Them, being, Eliphaz, Bildad, and Zophar but Elihu was not given the same opportunity to receive forgiveness. He had already been dealt with according to his folly [foolishness].

Job 42:7-9 NKJV And so it was, after the LORD had spoken these words to Job, that the LORD said to Eliphaz the Temanite, "My wrath is aroused against you and your two friends, for you have not spoken of Me what is right, <u>as My servant Job has</u>. 8 Now *therefore, take for yourselves seven bulls and seven rams, go to My servant Job, and offer up for yourselves a burnt offering; and My servant Job shall pray for you. For I will accept him, lest I deal with you according to your folly; because you have not spoken of Me what is right, <u>as My servant Job has</u>". So Eliphaz the Temanite and Bildad the Shuhite and Zophar the Naamathite went and did as the LORD commanded them; for the LORD had accepted Job.*

Going back, if God was indeed talking to Job from the very beginning when He showed up then that would mean He never dealt with Elihu, who was on the same side as Job's three friends—but the worst of them. Eliphaz, Bildad, and Zophar would have needed forgiveness for much less of an offense when compared to Elihu. However, Elihu would have walked away with no chastisement from God whatsoever.

As I stated earlier, and as can be clearly seen, being the worst of the four, God dealt with Elihu first. For him who dared to elevate himself to the level of God there was not given a chance for repentance.

Ultimately, in the end, everything Job had lost was restored to him and more. During Job's tribulation he was wrongly accused by his friends. They did not understand what was happening in the heavenly realm nor did they understand God. Sadly, to this day, although we have the benefit of seeing what had happened in the heavenly realm, Job is still wrongly accused. How much worse are we than Job's three friends?

In truth, Job should be recognized as one the greats, if not the greatest hero of the Bible. His name should be honored among the likes of people like Abraham, Isaac, Jacob, Ester, King David, Solomon, Mary, etc.

Unbeknownst to Job, he stood tall on behalf of all mankind. He proved the devil wrong, thus showing that true worshippers serve God out of love and obedience, not because of what they stand to gain.

Instead of Job being recognized for his devotion, steadfast faith, commitment, unwillingness to turn his back on God no matter what; and for standing up for all mankind, to this day, Job is barely mentioned. When he is spoken of, his words are met with criticism, and his actions with judgment. Now, just as then, we do not speak what is right as Job did.

For those who cannot get their head wrapped around the truth that Job did nothing wrong, and still feel he must have had some guilt, some fault that God punished him for; listen again to what God said in reference to Job's tribulations.

Job 2:3 NKJV Then the LORD said to Satan, "Have you considered My servant Job, that there is none like him on the earth, a blameless and upright man, one who fears God and shuns evil? And still, he holds fast to his integrity, although you incited Me against him, to destroy him WITHOUT CAUSE.

I think it is time we stop standing on the side of Job's three friends and Elihu who gave ungodly counsel; were chastising, condemning and scorning Job. We need to finally acknowledge he was not only blameless but stood tall for all mankind. He was also faithful to God and deserves our admiration and much gratitude.

Psa 1:1 Blessed is the man that walketh not in the counsel of the ungodly, nor standeth in the way of the sinner, nor sitteth in the seat of the scornful.

Revelations from Genesis
The Untold Biblical Story of Creation
Who Cain Feared and Where They Came From

So why do so many teach stories in scripture incorrectly, and yet, the members of the body do not catch it? Something as clear as the building of the ark and the story of creation should have been easily caught. Yet even today, while non-believers are not sure which came first, the chicken or the egg, some believers still are not sure whether or not the six days of creation were six literal days or six thousand years. Why? Could it be because we do not study the Word prayerfully?

Let me just take a minute to settle both questions once and for all. The chicken came first, and creation was in six literal days.

Without studying, we are susceptible to believing almost whatever it is we are taught, so long as it sounds biblical. Yet much of what we are taught was handed down over the years, and some of it is just not biblically accurate. Most of it is, mind you, but some of it is not. We cannot hold others responsible for what we believe. The Bible tells us that we must study to show ourselves approved by God.

2Ti 2:15 Study to show thyself approved unto God, a workman that needeth not to be ashamed, rightly dividing the word of truth.

We are to be believers that are not ashamed of the gospel and capable of rightly dividing [correctly understanding and expounding on the scriptures of] God's Word.

Now, most of us read the scriptures the same way when it is a story we believe we already know. Subconsciously, since we know the story already, we tend not to reread it with the intention of learning something new. We read it with the attitude of just reacquainting ourselves with the story as we remember it. This is most certainly the wrong attitude to have, as it blinds us from new revelations.

Not only is the Bible inexhaustible, but as we have established, we may have been taught incorrectly or simply misunderstood what it was we read. Therefore, our understanding of the story may be wrong, or at least some elements of it. Besides, there is always more to learn about a given story.

Instead of reading with the attitude that we know a particular story, what we should do, every time we read, is ask the Holy Spirit to either give us the correct understanding—or teach us a new lesson from the story. That way we can correctly apply it to our lives or simply understand the event as it was.

Now I am not talking about when you are studying. That is a different animal altogether. When you are just spending time in the word, it is important to always have the mindset that we may not, and in fact, will not ever, on this side of heaven, know everything there is to know—even with the simplest of stories.

When we are humble, understanding that we do not know all the lessons being taught in a given story, we are then open to learning more. Allowing the Holy Spirit to teach us and/or correct the things we understood incorrectly is paramount to understanding the scriptures.

Assuming the reason you are reading this book is because you are curious, and want to know who or what it was Cain feared; and where his wife came from is actually my case and point. You see, you have probably read the story of creation more than a few times, and even though the scriptures clearly tell us what Cain's fear was and where his wife came from, you do not know.

This is because every time you read the Genesis account, you read it from a place of already knowing the story based on what you were taught or believe you read. So then, every time you re-read it, you were just casually reacquainting yourself with it as opposed to having the mindset of reading it again to learn something new. Our minds subconsciously just ignore the verses that actually challenge what we believe, but since we know the Genesis account, or at least think we do, we never stopped to consider what it was we read.

For instance, when we read a certain scripture in Genesis 5, that we will be visiting later, that states, (...and blessed him, and called his name Adam), we never bat an eye because that is common knowledge. We already know God created a man out of the dust of the earth, blessed him, and called him Adam. Ok, nothing new there, we know that already. Until we read it with our eyes wide open and notice that is not what it says at all.

It actually says, (...and blessed them, and called their name Adam), not 'his name, their name.' That's right, that particular scripture does not say, 'God call him Adam.' The scripture says God called them Adam, which begins to paint a very different picture. We just never paid any attention to it because we know what we know, and that is God created Adam and then later created Eve. But why, why does the scripture say, "God called their name Adam?"

Does that not require further investigation? Should it not at least have piqued your curiosity? We simply ignored that statement and subconsciously read it as God called Adam, Adam. Again, since we know what we know, we just moved on without a second thought.

Know that every time you read God's word is an opportunity to learn something new. Always pray before reading and ask the Father to teach you what He has for you that day.

Hopefully, after you have read this book, you will never read the scriptures with the wrong mindset again!

So does the Bible tell us who or what it was Cain feared? If he was indeed fearful of other people, does the Bible tell us who they were and where they came from? Does it also tell us where his wife came from?

Not only is the answer to these questions yes, but what Moses actually told us about creation that we completely missed will shock you. First, however, you need to be disabused of the information you have about creation so that you can accurately read Genesis, again, for the first time.

Now I am certainly not saying we need to erase all that we know about creation so that we can learn something new. Instead we should expect to build upon what we already know and be willing to let the Holy Spirit tear down those things that are not correct. That is so we can fully understand the scriptures and the many lessons and messages behind them. When the Holy Spirit starts teaching you, you will hardly want to put the Bible down.

Understanding the creation story:

1.) If someone told you both males and females were created from the dust of the earth, you would immediately say that is not so. You would most certainly cite the fact that Eve was created from Adam's rib, not the dust of the earth.

2.) If someone told you that both males and females were not only created from the dust of the earth but also created at the same time, and on the same day; again, you would say that is not so either, as God said, "it is not good that man should be alone" and then He created Eve.

3.) If someone also told you that when God told man he could eat of every fruit bearing tree, it was without any restrictions whatsoever. You would say that too is not true, because God told Adam not to eat of the tree in the midst of the garden.

You will be surprised to know that in all three cases, you would be wrong. Yes, all three statements are true. Both males and females were indeed created from the dust of the earth, and at the same time, on the sixth day of creation. Also, God did indeed state they could eat of every tree and did not place any restrictions on them as to which trees they could not eat from.

Now you may argue that this is some new teaching not written in scripture, so it must be teachings from alternate sources. Well, while this may indeed be new, to you, it is only so because you, like me, were taught incorrectly to begin with—but no, it is not from alternate sources. It is clearly stated in your Bible, and of course we will be going over all those verses so that we can understand the scriptures for what it says, and not for what we think it says.

Again, we will be going over all the scriptures that show you exactly what I stated without any ambiguity. Also some additional extremely minor points with very little but justifiable conjecture and inference's which we can draw; but first you need to do something. You need to put this book down, pick up your Bible and read the creation story over again. With those three questions in mind, ask our Father to help you see those verses that you may have always glossed over more clearly.

Do not just read over it like you have in the past. When you come to a verse that seems to challenge what you know, stop and consider it. Pray about it and ask our Father to give you the proper understanding.

For instance, you will read that God said, "I have given you every herb bearing seed, which is upon the face of all the earth and every tree, in the which is the fruit of a tree yielding seed; to you, it shall be for meat." Consider that statement. Ask yourself why there are no restrictions there. Is it just because there was no garden at that point or is there more to it? Do not just assume you know what it means and do not skip pass verses that challenge what you believe.

Search the scriptures, because there are only putative contradictions and gaps that need to be filled, however, those contradictions and gaps only appear to be so because we do not know what we should know.

Of course there will always be things we do not yet understand, and that is why we will always be learning, but here I am referring solely to the creation story. Something we should all know or at least know the basic story of. Yet, even the basics we do not fully understand and so we believe a creation story that, for all intent and purposes, is not even recorded in scripture.

Once you are done reading the story of creation then come back and see if this book then lines up with what the Holy Spirit shows you.

So now let us dive into the scriptures and see what it was Cain was in fear of.

Assuming you went back and read the creation story, I will just summarize it. So God created Heaven and the earth. He created light and separated it from the darkness. He separated the waters from the waters. Gathered the waters into seas and formed the dry land. He created the grass of the fields, the herbs and the trees. He created the planets (stars), the moon and the sun, the fish of the sea and the fowl of the air. Blessed them and said "be fruitful and multiply..." He created the cattle, creeping things and beasts of the earth, and then He said, "let us make man in our image," and so He created man.

There is so much in just the first chapter of Genesis that you really have to take into account in order to clear your mind of your preconceived misinformation. Not only what was done and what was said but also what was not done and what was not said.

What was done:

What God did when creating sea life, in particular, was make it in abundance.

Gen1:21 KJV states: *And God created great whales, and every living creature that moveth, which the waters brought forth abundantly, after their kind, and every winged fowl after his kind: and God saw that it was good.*

What was not done:

God did not create just two whales, and two of every other sort of sea creature, the Bible tells us they were created in abundance. This is a notable point, and we'll see why later. Additionally, we will also see why it is reasonable to assume that the land animals, the cattle and beast, were created in pairs, the male and the female.

What was said:

Gen 1:26 KJV And God said, Let us make man in our image, after our likeness: and let them have dominion over the fish of the sea, and over the fowl of the air, and over the cattle, and over all the earth, and over every creeping thing that creepeth upon the earth.

What was not said:

God did not say, let us make (a) man in our image…

During creation the only thing the Bible states God made one of was the earth, heaven, moon, and sun. Everything else was created in multiples at the moment of creation, and in the case of sea creatures and the fowl of the air, many multiples.

This was no different when he created man. Stop and think for a moment. Could the idea of only creating one man have been the plan if man was to be fruitful and multiply like the rest of creation? Yes, we know Eve was to come later, but that was only after God stated, "it is not good that man should be alone," yet, even that statement is misunderstood and later we will show why that is. What you need to do now is ask yourself the following extremely important point question. When did God give man the command to be fruitful and multiply? Was it prior to or after the creation of Eve. If it was indeed prior to the creation of Eve then we most certainly must have missed something. We will come back to this point also.

So God said, "let us make man in our image." The pivotal question here is; was God talking about creating an individual person or mankind, consisting of both males and females? This is the ultimate question, and we will see why God was referring to creating people and could only have been referring to people as opposed to an individual person.

The original Hebrew text in this passage uses the word [(אָדָם) (Adam)] SAC [SBLB – H120 meaning: human being, man, mankind (much more frequently intended sense in OT), Adam, first man, city in Jordan valley]. It can also be translated as (man of the ground, red man, or humanity).

In order to determine which translation of the word [(אָדָם) (Adam)] is to be applied can be determined by the pronoun used and further backed up by the context in which the word is used. Since God then states, "and let them have dominion." the pronoun being the word 'them,' let's us know that in this context, God is referring to 'man' in the plural sense. Therefore, the only translation for the Hebrew word [(אָדָם) (Adam)] that can be applied to this verse would also have to be in the plural sense.

To further confirm God was referring to man in the plural sense we can translate the word 'Adam' in the singular form and see if the verse still makes sense.

Referring to man in the singular form the verse would read this way:

Gen 1: 26 Then God said, "Let us make (a) man in our image, according to our likeness; and let them have dominion over the fish of the sea, and over the birds of the air, and over the cattle, and over all the earth and over every creeping thing that creeps on the earth."

Referring to an individual as 'them' is not the proper way to understand the passage. This translation would render the verse senseless unless you start making further changes in order to make it conform to what you believe. Then you would have to rewrite the verse in this manner:

Gen 1: 26 Then God said, "Let us make (a) man in our image, according to our likeness; and let (him) have dominion over the fish of the sea, over the birds of the air, and over the cattle, over all the earth and over every creeping thing that creeps on the earth."

This is the very act of making the Bible conform to what we are already inclined to believe. Yet, there are really only two ways to read this scripture correctly, which would be to understand the word 'man' as humanity or mankind, and so the verse as originally written actually reads in the form of one of the following translations.

Gen 1: 26 KJV Then God said, "Let us make humanity in our image, according to our likeness; and let them have dominion over the fish of the sea, and over the birds of the air, and over the cattle, and over all the earth and over every creeping thing that creepth upon the earth."

Or

Gen 1: 26 KJV Then God said, "Let us make mankind in our image, according to our likeness; and let them have dominion over the fish of the sea, and over the birds of the air, and over the cattle, and over all the earth and over every creeping thing that creepth upon the earth."

It simply cannot be understood any other way without changing the scriptures. Understanding the Bible was originally written in three different languages, Hebrew, some Aramaic, and Greek, is important in translating it correctly. Knowing which parts of the Bible were originally written in what language is paramount in that endeavor.

However, the only translation we do not need is someone or some group's opinion, and the notion that God only created one man on the sixth day is just that; someone's opinion. That opinion, however, cannot be backed up by scripture while the fact that God created mankind in the beginning, and not just a single person is backed up by the scriptures—and there is lots of proof to that fact.

When we understand Gen 5:1-2 as the creation of mankind and not just an individual man, everything else about creation is made more clear. Moses clearly tells us that when God created mankind, He created males and females, on the same day and called their name Adam.

Gen 5:1-2 KJV This is the book of the generations of Adam. In the day that God created man, in the likeness of God made He him,
2. Male and Female created He them and blessed them, and called their name Adam in the day they were created.

Note that Gen 5:2 states: "Male and female created He **them** and blessed **them** and called **their** name **Adam**, in **the day they were created**. Every pronoun in this verse is pointing to multiple people having been created and on the same day.

Clearly, Moses is telling us that God created humanity male and female, just as He did with all the other creatures He created, and not just an individual man, and He called **their** name Adam (mankind). Had God created just an individual person, Moses would have recorded Gen 5:1-2 in this way:

Gen 5:1-2 This is the book of the generations of Adam. In the day that God created (him), in the likeness of God made He him. 2. (Male created He him) and blessed (him) and called (his) name Adam in the day (he) was created.

So let us pause for a minute and really give this some serious thought. The Bible states that God created mankind male and female at the same time on the same day. Yet we are taught God only created one man. Stop and really give this some thought. Ask yourself this question: why is it that to believe what we were taught, that God only created one man, requires us to ignore, overlook and even change scripture? While understanding He created mankind only requires us to read the scriptures as written by Moses? So who's account of creation should we believe; Moses' or the translators?

Now, as a side note, Gen 1:27 & 5 :1 also clearly shows that God is masculine, wherein He created mankind male and female but 'in His own image <u>created He him</u>,' the male. This is also emphasized in First Corinthians.

1 Cor 11:7 KJV For a man indeed ought not to cover his head, forasmuch as he is the image and glory of God: but the woman is the glory of the man.

This is how we are to correctly understand Gen 5:1-2 when translated from the original Hebrew text.

Gen 5:1-2 KJV This is the book of the generations of mankind. In the day that God created humanity, in the likeness of God made He him. 2. Male and female created He them and blessed them, and called their name mankind in the day they were created.

There is no other way to understand that passage of scripture because it is plainly written. The scripture is not being rewritten here, only rightly divided. Moses makes it very clear that both males and females were created at the same time on the same day and makes that statement twice.

Gen 5:1-2 clearly states: "in the **day** that God created man (mankind)" and "in the **day** they were created." Note when the bible repeats a statement or a word, it is telling you to take note of something important, something that is settled even. So here the Word is telling us to take note that both male and female where created on the same day, and what day was mankind created? The sixth day!

Now after God created mankind, he told them to be fruitful and multiply.

Gen 1:28 KJV And God blessed them, and God said unto them, be fruitful and multiply and replenish (fill) the earth and subdue it; and have dominion over the fish of the sea and over the fowl of the air and over every living thing that moveth upon the earth.

Are you getting this? The Bible says that God blessed **them** and said to **them...**, Now consider for a moment that God was simply talking to Adam, the individual, understanding Eve had not yet been created. No matter how you rewrote this verse, you could not get it to make sense. Again, understanding only Adam the individual was created on the sixth day the verse would say the following:

Gen 1:28 And God blessed (him), and God said unto (him), be fruitful and multiply and replenish (fill) the earth and subdue it; and have dominion over the fish of the sea and over the fowl of the air and over every living thing that moveth upon the earth.

Why would God want to confuse Adam by commanding him to do the one thing he would clearly be unable to do? Be fruitful and multiply? Are we to believe, only later, when God returned to earth on the eighth day, that He realized His error and said, "oops, My mistake, I did not realize I had only created the one man and told him to multiply?" God was clearly talking to mankind and giving them the same instructions he gave to all the other creatures He created; to "be fruitful and multiply." Now it is not recorded that God told the cattle to be fruitful and multiply but is either implied or it requires further study.

Seeing as how Adam would have been extremely confused after being given those instructions, stop for a moment and do something you may not have done before when reading this passage. Stop and consider what God did and what God said. Did He really create one man and tell him to be fruitful and multiply? Or did He give those instructions to mankind? Again, as mentioned earlier, it is extremely important to note that Eve was not yet created when Adam was given the command to be fruitful and multiply.

To believe God was talking to an individual requires more than just changing the scriptures. It means you would have to change your whole understanding of science, biology, and procreation. It is just not sensible to conclude that God was talking to just one man and gave him instructions to be fruitful and multiply as though God Himself was not fully committed to how He wanted procreation to function when it came to mankind.

Still, I know it is hard to let go of this notion of a single individual being created but in order to make the creation story conform to your view point you have to translate the entire story this way:

*Gen 1:26, 31KJV And God said, Let us make **a** man in our image, after our likeness: and let **him** have dominion over the fish of the sea, and over the fowl of the air, and over the cattle, and over all the earth, and over every creeping thing that creepeth upon the earth.*

*27 So God created **a** man in His own image, in the image of God created He him; male ~~and female~~ created He **him**.*

*28 And God blessed **him**, and God said unto him, ~~Be fruitful and multiply, and replenish the earth, and subdue it: and~~ have dominion over the fish of the sea and over the fowl of the air, and over every living thing that moveth upon the earth.*

29 And God said, behold, I have given you every herb bearing seed, which is upon the face of all the earth, and every tree, in the which is the fruit of the tree yielding seed; to you, it shall be for meat.

30 And to every beast of the earth, and to every fowl of the air, and to every thing that creepeth upon the earth, wherein there is life, I have given every green herb for meat; and it was so.

31 And God Saw every thing that He had made, and, behold, it was very good. And the evening and the morning were the sixth day.

This rewriting of scripture scores a ten in Bible Gymnastics!

All trees where allowed for food without restriction.

Gen 1:29 KJV And God said, behold, I have given you every herb bearing seed, which is upon the face of all the earth and every tree, in the which is the fruit of a tree yielding seed. To you, it shall be for meat.

Gen 1:29 NKJV And God said, see, I have given you every herb that yields seed which is on the face of all the earth, and every tree whose fruit yields seed; to you, it shall be for food.

Notice what was not said:

God did not say they could eat of every tree, with the exception of any particular tree. God said **'every'** fruit tree was for food, and He made **no exceptions**, not one, and placed **no restrictions**.

Now, of course, some will argue that there were no exceptions because the tree of life & the tree of the knowledge of good and evil were not yet on earth. However, accepting that assumption for the only basis of there being no restrictions as fact requires you to ignore everything else. Additionally, the reason why there were no exceptions is given by God; only it has to be unearthed, and we will get to that shortly.

Gen 1:31 KJV And God saw everything that he had made and behold it was very good, and the evening and the morning were the sixth day.

Now let this really sink in. At this point, creation is complete; everything is done with nothing left to create. The earth is formed, the creatures are created, and with the exception of sea life and possibly the fowl of the air, in the case of every creature created on the earth, they were all made from the dust of the earth.

Both the male and female of every species were created and given the same instructions. 'This is what you are to eat, and you are to be fruitful and multiply.' There was no reason or excuse for any of God's creation, not even mankind having been given the same command, to not be fruitful and multiply. All of God's creation was set and capable of obeying God's commands.

God had finished His work, and the Bible tells us that all the host of them was finished. Not some of them, not even most of them but all of them were completed. Then on the seventh day God rested from all His work. Once again, note that after God was completely finished with creation there is no mention of Eve, yet man was to multiply.

Gen 2:1-3 KJV Thus the heavens and the earth were finished and all the host of them 2. And on the seventh day, God ended His work which He had made, and He rested on the seventh day from all His work which He had made 3. And God blessed the seventh day and sanctified it because that in it he had rested from all His work which God created and made.

So we need to understand that God created all He wanted to create in six days, and it was FINISHED. If God had only created one man, how could it be declared that creation was finished? Creation could not have been declared finished if there was only one man on the earth because one man could not multiply. Creation could only have been declared finished with the creation of mankind not an individual man. Once mankind was created, then, and only then, could the declaration of a finished work be made.

Simply put, on the last day, God formed his crowning creation, mankind. He blessed them and gave them dominion over everything else He had created, and He told them to be fruitful and multiply and fill the earth. The Bible makes no bones about that and says so absent of any ambiguity. The fact that creation was declared finished prior to the creation of Eve should not go unnoticed.

Nothing more was needed for any of God's creation to fulfill the commandment given to them. Had God rested for a thousand years after the sixth day of creation before He returned to the earth, all of His creation would have flourished. Both man, beast, and creeping things would have been well on the way to filling the earth.

Now pay close attention to this verse that may seem insignificant to the case I am making but in fact is actually very significant.

Gen 1:31 KJV And God saw everything that He had made, and behold; it was very Good...

God created mankind from the dust of the ground, both male and female were created at the same time and given the same instructions. Every fruit bearing tree and herb bearing seed was for food, and after He was finished with all of creation, God said, "it was **very good.**" What is very significant here is that after each day of creation, with the exception of the first and second day, God said it was good. However, on the sixth day, God said it was **very good,** and we will come back to this very important point.

After God had rested and hallowed the seventh day and sanctified it, we will see the first time God the Father separates, calls out from mankind, His chosen, and result of that separation is then declared **not good**.

Gen 2:8 KJV And the Lord God planted a garden eastward in Eden; and there put He the man whom He had formed.

The garden was planted after God was finished with creation and after he had rested from all his work. God came back down to earth on what was most likely the eighth day, and planted a garden, then separated Adam from the others He created. The Bible says God put 'the man' who He had formed. This word for man cannot be translated to mankind, only as an individual person.

Gen 2:16-17 KJV And the Lord God commanded 'the man' saying , of every tree of the garden thou mayest freely eat: 17. but of the tree of the knowledge of good and evil, thou shalt not eat of it; for in the day that thou eatest thereof, thou shalt surely die.

So here we see God talking to one man, Adam, the first of the creation of mankind who was given the name of mankind. Once God separated him from mankind, He then gave Adam different instructions from what was given when first instructed with the others as to what was permissible to eat.

God separated, called out, His chosen from mankind, and gave him special instructions. God's chosen are to live differently and even eat differently from the others. At the time of creation, mankind was told that every tree was for food, but once Adam is separated from mankind, God tells him there is now an exception to what he can eat.

Gen 2:18 KJV And the Lord God said, it is not good that the man should be alone, I will make a help, meet for him.

WAIT A MINUTE, STOP THE PRESS!

Did God just realize He had told Adam to be fruitful and multiply, but He forgot to create a female? Did God just realize that Adam was alone? Going back to the point I made earlier about the importance of God declaring certain days as good, not others.

Again, there were only two other times God did not say the day was good. That was on day one and day two. On day one, when He separated the light from the darkness, and on day two, when He separated the waters from the waters. For argument sake, yes, God did say it was good on day one, but He was only referring to the light he spoke into existence; He saw that the light was good. Once He separated the light from the darkness, the day was not declared good, as with the second day when He separated the waters. That day was not declared as good either.

It just may be that God does not view separation as good. Which is why on day one and day two, where they ended in separation, it was not declared good, and now, on what was possibly the eighth day, when He separated Adam from Adam [Adam the man from Adam (mankind)] that separation was declared not good.

Now there was separation on day four, but it was connected to day one in that it was concerning the separation of night and day, which were already divided, so there was really no new separation occurring; and so day four of creation was declared good.

After the sixth and finally day of creation, God said it was very good. So, let this sink in; why would God then say it was not good that Adam should be alone on the eighth day if he was already alone from the sixth day when God declared it was not only good but very good? This is a question that simply cannot be overlooked, and the simple answer is this; because Adam was not alone on day six of creation, as the Bible clearly states God made mankind not just an individual man.

Now on the eighth day, God acknowledges that Adam was alone, being separated from the rest of mankind, and declared his new condition as not good, so God set out to find a helper, and companion for him.

WAIT A MINUTE, STOP THE PRESS ONE MORE TIME!

If we are to believe that God only created Adam and then rested on the seventh day, we must also believe that God made the following mistakes:
[Mistake Number One]
God created Adam by himself and gave him the command to be fruitful and multiply.

[Mistake Number Two]

After finishing creation, He declared it was very good, only to return and plant a garden where He put the man, and then realized it was not so good after all because Adam was all alone. Obviously, this would hinder him from being fruitful and multiplying.

[Mistake Number Three]

After recognizing mistake number one, making it impossible for man to multiply. Then recognizing mistake number two, stating His finished creation was very good then having to take it back. God then makes yet another mistake by bringing him the animals to find him a suitable companion in order to fix the mistakes— which instead of fixing all the mistakes would only serve to further compound them.

This just cannot be. God making one mistake, ok I get it, nobody's perfect. God making three compounding mistakes, how could that happen? Yes, I am being facetious. Of course God does not make mistakes.

So, looking at it from the viewpoint of God only creating one man, instead of providing Adam with a female so that he could do as God commanded, and actually procreate and fill the earth—it appears God set out to find a pet for him. One to accompany him, and to be a helper to him throughout the day.

God was obviously not concerned with mankind, who was given dominion over the earth, not having the capability of filling the earth. The truth is His only concern was that having separated Adam he was lonely throughout the day when God was not with him, so providing a companion was the answer. God was not seeking to fix a mistake only to resolve a newly created issue, Adam's loneliness.

Clearly, when God said, "it is not good that man should be alone," it was not because he would not be able to fill the earth but because he was no longer with mankind. He was all by himself. However, if it were that God realized that Adam could not fulfill the commandment given to be fruitful and multiply, then obviously, God would have sought to provide a female for Adam and not a pet. The only reason why the Father was in no hurry to find Adam a wife, was because the filling of the earth would have been left to those outside the garden.

So to understand the scripture correctly, with us conforming to the word, let us read the entirety of the sixth day of creation as written in the original Hebrew correctly translated and note how there is no need to add or remove words. No verses need to be taken out. Just two words correctly translated.

*Gen 1:26, 31KJV And God said, Let us make **mankind** in our image, after our likeness: and let them have dominion over the fish of the sea, and over the fowl of the air, and over the cattle,* and over all the earth, and over every creeping thing that creepeth upon the earth.

27 So God created **mankind** in His own image, in the image of God created He him; male and female created He them.

28 And God blessed them, and God said unto them, Be fruitful and multiply, and replenish the earth, and subdue it: and have dominion over the fish of the sea and over the fowl of the air, and over every living thing that moveth upon the earth.

29 And God said, behold, I have given you every herb bearing seed, which is upon the face of all the earth, and every tree, in the which is the fruit of the tree yielding seed; to you, it shall be for meat.

30 And to every beast of the earth, and to every fowl of the air, and to every thing that creepeth upon the earth, wherein there is life, I have given every green herb for meat; and it was so.

31 And God Saw every thing that He had made, and, behold, it was very good. And the evening and the morning were the sixth day.

Note there is zero ambiguity there. The creation of mankind is extremely clear, needing no interpretation just the proper understanding of the Hebrews words used.

Gen 2:18-20 KJV And the Lord God said, it is not good that the man should be alone, I will make a help meet for him. 19. And out of the ground the Lord God formed every beast of the field [not something He was doing right then but just re-establishing from where the beast came] *and every fowl of the air and brought them unto Adam to see what he would call them; and whatsoever Adam called every living creature, that was the name thereof. 20. And Adam gave names to all cattle and to the fowl of the air, and to every beast of the field, but for Adam, there was not found an help meet for him.*

So no helper or companion was found for Adam, and yet God did not go and take a female from the others outside the garden. What God did was something completely different. For the first and only time in creation, God created a life using a part of another life. No other creature was created this way, neither man nor beast.

Gen 2:21 KJV And the Lord God caused a deep sleep to fall upon Adam, and he slept: and He took one of his ribs and closed up the flesh instead thereof; 22. and the rib, which the Lord God had taken from man He made a woman and brought her unto the man.

Note God did not say the same thing as He did on the sixth day. He did not refer to Eve, as she would be later named, as just a female. This creation was created differently from the rest of mankind, and Adam later also acknowledges this fact.

Gen 2:23 KJV And Adam said, this is <u>now</u> bone of my bones and flesh of my flesh: she shall be called <u>Woman</u> because she was taken out of Man.

Because of our misunderstanding, when we read this verse, we understood Adam stated, "this is now bone of my bone...," because it was the first time he was seeing a female, but this is not so. He makes this statement because, unlike the other females, Eve was not made of the dust of the ground; she was created out of the wound of a man. Adam clearly acknowledging this difference gives this female a new distinction, 'woman.'

The Hebrew word for female is (נקבה, neqebah) **SAC.** This is the word used when God first created mankind; but here, Adam uses the word (אשה, ishshah) **SAC**, declaring Eve's difference from the other females.

Adam was the first man created from the dust of the earth and only male placed in the garden, and now Eve would be the first and the only female created out of man and not directly out of dust and placed in the garden.

Gen 3:20 KJV And Adam called his wife's name Eve because she was the mother of all living.

This misunderstood verse has served to fuel the idea that there was only the two of them, but this was not a matter of fact at that time, but rather a prophetic statement Adam made.

What he was prophesying was that Eve would be the mother of all living, since at the time Adam named Eve she had not yet given birth to any child. He could not have meant she was currently the mother of all living as she had only just come into being. However, after the advent of the flood, Eve would indeed be the mother of all living. Not that Adam knew there would be a flood, and only his descendants would survive, mind you.

Remember, I stated that some scholars concluded that Cain married either a sister or niece. The root of this misunderstanding also comes from Gen 3:20, where Adam called his wife's name Eve, because she was the mother of all living. Again, this is because they had not gotten the proper understanding which was just established.

Not that the scriptures need to be cleared up or interpreted so that it is easier to understand. It is only because of decades of incorrect teaching that have blinded people from the proper understanding that it needs to be shown in the proper light. That being said, there are some hidden things in scripture that have to be dug out in order to get a deeper understanding.

Again, some scholars and others concluded who Cain feared was his siblings or even the descendents of Abel who may have wanted revenge for their father's murder. Remember, this is not at all possible and once again requires an exercise in Bible gymnastics in order to be explained.

First, the Bible makes no mention nor makes any inference that Abel was married, so why make up that he was? Second, Genesis 5:3 clearly states Adam's descendents and starts with Seth, who was his third son born after the death of Abel, and after Cain's exile and Adam did not have other sons nor daughters until after Seth, therefore there were no other siblings around for Cain to fear nor marry. This is a crucial fact when considering how Cain came to have a wife.

Gen 5:3-4 KJV And Adam lived an hundred and thirty years and begat a son in his own likeness, after his own image and called his name Seth. 4. And the days of Adam after he had begotten Seth were eight hundred years; and he begat sons and daughters.

Gen 4:25 KJV And Adam knew his wife again, and she bare a son and called his name Seth; for God, said she, hath appointed me another seed instead of Abel whom Cain slew.

When Cain was exiled, he left on his own, having no wife, no siblings, and therefore, no children. He left Adam and Eve childless having one dead son and himself in exile.

So, God sentenced Cain to be a fugitive and a vagabond. At first glance, this would make sense. He was exiled from his home to wander about on his own, which would make him a vagabond, and he committed murder which would make him a fugitive. However, the Hebrew words used here does not mean a fugitive in that sense, as in a fugitive of the law. Nor does it mean a vagabond in the sense of simply being a homeless wanderer.

The word God used for fugitive was (עו׳ , Nua) **SAC [SBLB – H5128** meaning: **to quiver, totter, shake, reel, stagger, wander, move, sift, make move, wave, waver, tremble].** And the word for Vagabond (ני׳, nûd) **SAC [SBLB H5110** meaning: **a primitive root; to nod, i.e. waver; figuratively, to wander, flee, disappear; also (from shaking the head in sympathy), to console, deplore, or (from tossing the head in scorn) taunt:—bemoan, flee, get, mourn, make to move, take pitty, remove, shake, skip for joy, be sorry, vagabond, way, wandering.**

So God sentence Cain to be a wandering wanderer; someone who walked alone aimlessly, constantly on the move bemoaning their actions that brought about their suffering. However, although Cain showed no remorse; thinking only of himself and bemoaning his punishment more than his actions, God instead showed Cain mercy and removed a portion of his punishment from him.

Cain's fear of being killed if found by others was what ensured he would be a wandering wanderer. In fact, when he shares with God his fear for his life if he should be found by others, God does not challenge nor correct Cain. He did not ask Cain what 'others' he was referring to. In fact, God understands his concern and offers him protection from the 'others', being those who were created from the beginning alongside Adam and their descendants.

Before God placed this protection on Cain, Cain knew he was destined to live for hundreds of years as a vagabond and a fugitive. He would not be able to associate with others for fear they would kill him.

Instead, God placed a mark on Cain less any of the others finding him should kill him, then vengeance would be taken on them seven-fold. If there were not other people beyond where Adam and Eve were, then who was God going to take vengeance on? The only other two people on earth, if your only understanding is the account taught for years, would have been Adam and Eve. Or did God just commit yet another error? I think not!

Cain would have been in fear of Adam and possibly Eve or future siblings, and God would have marked him so that if his parents or a sibling born down the road found him, they would see the mark and maybe not kill him for fear they would receive seven times worse. That is just not sensible.

What is also key to note here is once God placed this protection over Cain, his outlook became very different. He was no longer facing a life of solitude. Instead of being exiled and wandering the earth in solitude, hiding from others, he headed straight for the land where he knew people were.

So, instead of Moses ending the story of Cain with something along the lines of, 'and so Cain left his home and wandered the earth serving his punishment rendered by God.' We read a completely different story, wherein, Cain leaves his home and simply finds a home elsewhere. With God's protection Cain's greatest fears were all but erased. What Cain did not know, however, was that his sin would be visited on his descendants, and they would all be wiped off the earth during the great flood.

Gen 4: 16-17 KJV And Cain went out from the presence of the Lord and dwelt in the land of Nod, on the east of Eden. 17. And Cain knew his wife, and she conceived and bare Enoch, and he (Cain) builded a city and called the name of the city after the name of his son, Enoch.

Wait a minute! So let us say Cain did have a sister Moses forgot or chose not to mention. So having only a wife and son and no one else around, how and why would Cain build a city? Did he have other sons and daughters in his latter years, and then when they were old enough to work, use the younger children to build a city in honor of his first born, Enoch? Of course not; the inference here is that God still blessed Cain, and sometime after arriving in Nod he found a wife and became very wealthy in the land—and was able to build his own city in that land utilizing the labor of the inhabitants.

This is no different from the inference the Bible makes of Noah being extremely wealthy, as no poor person would have had the resources to hire workers to help build a giant ark. Not to mention stocking it with food to feed all the animals, and his family for over a year.

Additionally, it is extremely important to note that building a city would not likely be on the mind of a man who only had a wife and child; and the only other people he would have known to be alive were his mother and father, who were out west. It would have been an incredibly massive vision for a man having never seen a city, nor any more than a three other people to want to take on the incredible task of building a city. Not to mention a terribly hard, and senseless job for one man and his wife & child to undertake.

Build a house, sure, but a whole city. Why? Obviously, he was around people and plenty of them in that the people who were created alongside Adam were busy being fruitful and multiplying, as God had commanded them.

Now, it has been said that the word 'city' can mean a large house or home, so what Cain built was a house and named it after his first born, Enoch. This claim, however, is another exercise in

Bible gymnastics. The Hebrew word for city, [עִיר][eer] SBLB, does not translate to home or house. This word for city also appears one thousand ninety five times in the Bible and not once is it used to refer to a home or house. It always refers to a city as it is first mentioned in the scriptures.

The Hebrew word for home or house is, [בַּיִת] [bah'-yith] SBLB, and is used two thousand fifty six times in the Bible. If the scriptures were telling us that Cain built a home and not a physical city then out of a combined three thousand one hundred and fifty one uses, this would be the only time they used the wrong word.

Additionally, there is no other instance in the Bible where a house is built and named for a prominent person's child. It is always a city. Clearly, what Cain built was a city, and that fact, by itself, calls for a large population group.

So now we can clearly see who Cain feared when he was sent into exile from his family, and from the face of God. It was the people that were created from the beginning on day six but were left outside of the garden.

Now the following is speculation; but Cain may have seen and therefore met some of the others God created over the years seeing as he had never been in the Garden where no other people lived besides Adam and Eve. He was born and raised on the outside of the garden in Eden, where other people were his entire life.

It is quite possible they may have befriended and even traded with them. Again, it is just speculation, but there is no reason to think it was not so, especially since Cain knew exactly where to go to find people once he was afforded protection.

More conjecture, but could it be possible that Cain's fleeing to Nod after he murdered his brother was the impetus for or foreshadowing of the Israelites having to set up cities of refuge for accused murderers so they could escape punishment before they were afforded a trial?

Numbers 35:6-34 KJV And among the cities which ye shall give unto the Levites there shall be six cities for refuge, which ye shall appoint for the manslayer, that he may flee thither...

Certainly, I'm not asserting it was, just food for thought. What is truly sad, however, is that of all God's creation, the only one to disobey Him was the one creation He made in His own image, and gave control over the earth to. By giving mankind free will, man failed miserably.

Now once you've studied the scriptures for any period of time, you will find that sometimes individual words or phrases are repeated. Even stories in the Bible are often repeated, as I stated before. This is all significant and requires our attention. It may be different characters in different places or even the same places and sometimes even involve some of the same characters, but the story will be the same even though they may have variations. Only what is sometimes not clearly understood in one story is made clear in the other, due to those very variations.

The same goes for books in the Bible. If an event is not made clear or a verse is not clear in one book, there is another book, or another verse that will help to explain it. This is why the Bible needs no interpreter as it interprets itself.

So, is there another story of creation in the scriptures that further makes clear the fact that God created mankind and not just a man? Yes there is! In fact, this story is so close to the creation story it almost mirrors it. So, in conclusion, we will match up the parallel story that will show that God did not start creation with just one man.

Parallel story of creation

In the beginning, the earth was a mass of water.

After the flood, the earth was a mass of water.

In the beginning, God's spirit moved over the face of the waters.

After the flood, God caused a wind to move over the waters.

In the beginning, God caused the dry land to appear.

After the flood, God caused the dry land to appear.

In the beginning, God created the fish in the sea in abundance.

After the flood, there were fish in the sea in abundance.

In the beginning, God brought forth grass and the herb yielding seeds and fruit trees after the dry land appeared.

After the flood, came forth the grass and the herb yielding seed and the fruit trees after the dry land appeared.

In the beginning, the first creature on the earth was the fowl of the air.

After the flood, the first creature on earth was the fowl of the air.

In the beginning, the cattle and the beast of the field appeared after the fowl of the air.

After the flood, the cattle and the beast of the field appeared after the fowl of the air.

In the beginning, the beast of the field appeared on the earth before mankind.

After the flood, the beast of the field appeared on the earth before mankind.

In the beginning, God brought forth both male and female at the same time.

After the flood, out of the ark came forth both male and female at the same time.

In the beginning, God gave mankind instructions to be fruitful and multiply.

After the flood, God gave mankind instructions to be fruitful and multiply.

In the beginning, God gave mankind instructions as to what was food without exceptions.

After the flood, God gave mankind instructions as to what was food without exception.

In the beginning, after God called out His own and separated man, from man, he gave His called out one different instructions as to what was and was not allowable to eat.

After the flood, after God called out His own and separated man, from man, He gave His called out ones different instructions as to what was and was not allowable to eat.

To be clear:

In the beginning, God first instructed mankind that all fruit bearing trees and all the herbs of the field was for food. Then after He separated His chosen, Adam, from mankind, He placed a restriction and told him which fruit bearing tree he could not eat.

After the flood, God instructed mankind that all the animals were now included for food. Then after He separated His chosen people, the Hebrews, from mankind, He placed a restriction and told them which animals they could not eat.

Now there was an instruction to mankind, after the flood, not to eat flesh with the life blood in it. The blood, however, was never a source of food. Also this has a deeper meaning that this book is not meant to cover.

What is also notable is the following:

In the beginning, prior to the fall, God brought all the animals to man so that he could name them.

Prior to the flood, God brought all the animals to man so that he could save them.

Some may argue that God was simply just not going to start again, after the flood, with one man. However, when understood correctly, we can see from the scriptures that God never started out with one man. For centuries, we just told the story of creation as though He did. The people who Cain feared and who God warned against killing Cain by placing a sign on him, were the very same people and their descendants who were created from the beginning when God created mankind—but they lived outside the garden. The very same people created on the sixth day that God called Adam (mankind).

Now, in the beginning, God separated His chosen and placed him in the garden, then told him to obey; but now man has to first be obedient to the Father in order to get back into to the garden. Obedience is defined as accepting Jesus, God's son, as your Lord and Savior; and following God's ways all of your days. From the time God's chosen were exiled from the garden, He had put a plan in action to redeem His 'separated ones' and place them back in the garden to remain with Him there forever.

Only by accepting Yeshua/Jesus as your Lord and Savior and obeying the Father will you find the only door that leads us back into the garden, but not only His chosen but all those who are called and believe in the mighty name of Yeshua!

Milton Keynes UK
Ingram Content Group UK Ltd.
UKHW020326150823
426856UK00009B/54